A COMPLETE INTRODUCTION TO

GERBILS

Cinnamon and dove gerbils only three weeks old. Photo by M. Gilroy.

A COMPLETE INTRODUCTION TO

GERBILS

COMPLETELY ILLUSTRATED IN FULL COLOR

An albino gerbil in its typical upright pose. Photo by M. Gilroy.

Mrs. M. Ostrow

Distributed in the UNITED STATES by T.F.H. Publications, Inc., 211 West Sylvania Avenue, Neptune City, NJ 07753; in CANADA to the Pet Trade by H & L Pet Supplies Inc., 27 Kingston Crescent, Kitchener, Ontario N2B 2T6; Rolf C. Hagen Ltd., 3225 Sartelon Street, Montreal 382 Quebec; in CANADA to the Book Trade by Macmillan of Canada (A Division of Canada Publishing Corporation), 164 Commander Boulevard, Agincourt, Ontario M1S 3C7; in ENGLAND by T.F.H. Publications Limited, 4 Kier Park, Ascot, Berkshire SL5 7DS; in AUSTRALIA AND THE SOUTH PACIFIC by T.F.H. (Australia) Pty. Ltd., Box 149, Brookvale 2100 N.S.W., Australia; in NEW ZEALAND by Ross Haines & Son, Ltd., 18 Monmouth Street, Grey Lynn, Auckland 2 New Zealand; in SINGAPORE AND MALAYSIA by MPH Distributors (S) Pte., Ltd., 601 Sims Drive, #03/07/21, Singapore 1438; in the PHILIPPINES by Bio-Research, 5 Lippay Street, San Lorenzo Village, Makati Rizal; in SOUTH AFRICA by Multipet Pty. Ltd., 30 Turners Avenue, Durban 4001. Published by T.F.H. Publications Inc. Manufactured in the United States of America by T.F.H. Publications, Inc.

Contents

Above: *Gerbils (top photo) can be told from fancy rats and mice (bottom photos) by the blunter head, larger eye, and hairy tail ending in a tuft of hair. As more mutations of gerbils occur, more and more of the fancy rat and mouse patterns will appear in gerbils.*

Introduction

The desire to keep pairs of pets may have had its origin back in the time of Noah. Nearly everyone knows that Noah took aboard two of every animal (one male and one female) so that each species could re-establish itself after the great flood.

Today's pet-keeper, whether the pets are gerbils, hamsters, mice, rats, rabbits, guinea pigs, turtles, lizards, salamanders, guppies or goldfish, seems to feel some sort of moral obligation to provide each pet with a companion of the opposite sex. This naturally leads to propagation of the species, often without any extra encouragement from the pet-keeper. When the founders of the pet-keeper's "model population" consist of only one pair - and usually brother and sister, at that - it generally doesn't take very many pet generations for the pet-keeper to become discouraged due to the increasing weakness of each new generation. Then he either moves on to another kind of pet or gives up pet-keeping entirely. Noah obviously wasn't a geneticist or he would have known about the problems of inbreeding in starting a whole new population from only two founders.

If you have already purchased your gerbils or have definitely decided to purchase them, in all probability you will follow the precepts of our common ancient ancestor, Noah, and have one male and one female. This means that when they grow to maturation they will probably breed. Therefore, you might as well know something about their breeding habits so you can offer your gerbils a correct environment and give them the greatest chance to have normal, healthy offspring. That is the reason this book was written - to give you some solid ideas on how to breed and raise reasonably healthy gerbils, whether you are doing it for pure fun, for a school science project or perhaps even to make some money by large-scale breeding.

Introduction

No matter what your reason for breeding gerbils, a haphazard plan or no plan at all usually produces only haphazard results or no results. On the other hand, knowing something about gerbils - where they live, what they eat, how they mate, etc. - before embarking on a breeding plan will help you produce sturdier, better-looking gerbils. This in itself is an adequate reward for most gerbil lovers, but if you plan to make some money with your gerbils, hardy, attractive stock is indeed necessary to success.

It is not my intention in this book to pass on to you all of the fine details of gerbil behavior that I learned by living with several hundred of them in a laboratory eight hours a day for nearly two years. Rather, I intend to pick out the most important points, from my own experiences and from the experiences of others who have worked with gerbils as extensively or perhaps even more than I, and present that information in an easily understood manner with as little scientific jargon as possible.

The best way to breed an animal successfully is to understand as much as possible about that animal's natural history. That does not mean that it is necessary to replicate the animal's natural environment to be successful in breeding it. It is merely a way of learning what its tolerance levels are to the conditions you will subject it to in keeping it as a pet and breeding it. Therefore, a synopsis of the Mongolian gerbil's natural history as well as its environmental requirements will be presented before going into the details of its breeding habits.

Above: *Careful consideration should go into your gerbil purchase. If you choose a weak and colorless strain, they will cause you trouble when you try to breed them and you will not be able to sell or trade your duplicate stock. A strong, colorful strain, on the other hand, will be easier to breed and easier to trade. Photo by Dr. Herbert R. Axelrod.*

This Canadian white spot is showing one of the gerbil's most desirable traits: curiosity. Photo by M. Gilroy.

The Gerbil

Arid and semi-arid deserts of Africa, Asia and the Middle East are the natural homes of the rat-like animals that have come to be known as gerbils. There are many species of gerbils, and each one has a common name based either on its locality or on some of its outstanding physical features. For example, sand rats, fat-tailed mice, naked-soled gerbils, Jerusalem gerbils and Mongolian gerbils are the names of just a few of the more well-known species.

As in most speciose groups of organisms, the scientific categorization of gerbils has not been without its problems. The higher taxa are, of course, not in doubt. Gerbils are mammals of the order Rodentia and the family Cricetidae, the same family to which hamsters and field mice (true rats belong to the family Muridae) belong. There are several genera of gerbils, with *Meriones* being the most well-known. There are about 12 species belonging to this genus, and the Mongolian gerbil, *Meriones unguiculatus,* is without a doubt the best-known of them all. It is this

Above: *This gray mutant gerbil is still a member of the parent species,* Meriones unguiculatus. *Photo by M. Gilroy.*

species that is most commonly imported for sale in the pet trade and for experimental use in laboratories. This is also

The Gerbil

the species that is rapidly becoming highly domesticated and from which a few new color strains are being developed by commercial breeders. The Mongolian gerbil, except where noted, is the one described throughout this book.

Below: Most of the many other species of gerbils look much like the common Mongolian gerbil. This is a Gerbillus *species.*

Gerbils are generally rat-like in appearance but can be immediately distinguished from rats by the fur-covered tail - while the rat has a few scattered hairs on the tail, its tail is not fur-covered. Gerbils have grayish brown or reddish brown fur except on the underside, which tends to be whitish. The brown hairs have a pattern known as agouti that is typical of the coloration of most

Facing page: All common rodents share a very similar skeletal pattern, as can be seen by these skeletons of a hamster (top two photos) and a guinea pig (bottom two photos). A gerbil skeleton looks much like a hamster's but of course with a very long tail. Photos by Dr. Herbert R. Axelrod.

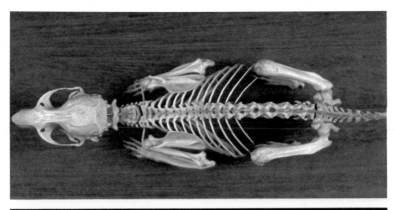

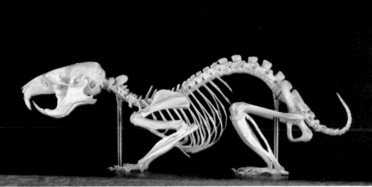

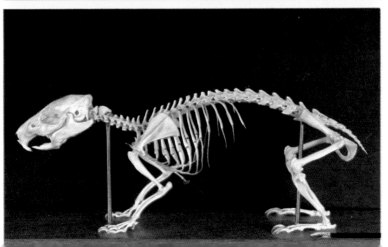

The common gerbil is still the typical brownish and off-white of the wild populations, a color scheme pleasing to many people. Photo by S. A. Thompson.

desert rodents (and many non-desert rodents as well). Most of the hairs of an agouti-colored animal are white at the base, have a tannish or yellowish center and are black at the tip. Interspersed among these shorter hairs are guard hairs which are thicker and stiffer than the

Left: *The pure white belly fur of a clean, well cared for gerbil shows up well here.*

Facing page: *Three of the newer gerbil colors: a black flanked by a cinnamon and a Canadian white spot. Photo by M. Gilroy.*

multicolored hairs and are usually black. The distribution of the guard hairs and the distribution of color on each of the softer hairs are what determine the gerbil's overall color. Agouti coloration helps the gerbil blend in with its background, which makes it less subject to predation.

A male adult Mongolian gerbil has a length from the tip of the length of nearly ten inches, but these are rarely seen in captivity. The mature Mongolian gerbil's tail is straight and about as long as its body. It is fur-covered and tends to be tufted at the tip. The gerbil's forelimbs are relatively small compared to the hindlimbs. The hindlegs

snout to the base of the tail of about four inches and weighs nearly four ounces. Females are usually just a bit smaller. There are some gerbil species that grow to a and hindfeet are greatly enlarged. The limb structure enables the gerbil to be a skillful jumper and allows it to sit up on the hindlimbs, thus freeing the

forelimbs for other
purposes such as food
manipulation, which it
does in a squirrel-like
manner.

Although gerbils are
found in low-lying plains,
arid steppes,

Left: *This young gerbil has
already learned to use its hands
to manipulate its food. Photo by
M. Gilroy.*

Facing page: *Gerbils are
animals of low-lying plains and
grasslands, a fact reflected in
their preference for open areas
in the cage.*

grasslands, cultivated
fields and mountain
valleys, their most
typical habitats are the
sparsely scattered,
somewhat bushy areas
of clay and sand
deserts. As is typical of

Above: *Nothing seems to interest a gerbil more than a tunnel, even if it is just the long tube of cardboard from the middle of a roll of paper towels. Photo by D. G. Robinson, Jr.*

most desert mammals, gerbils have extremely keen hearing which results from well-developed auditory or otic bullae (the part of the skull that houses the brain's acoustical center). The rat's brain has greatly enlarged olfactory lobes, and anatomists often refer to it as the "primitive smell brain." In a similar way, the gerbil's brain might be called a "sound brain" because of its enlarged otic structures and the gerbil's strongly sound-oriented

Above: the gerbil's fine sense of smell helps it discriminate sunflower seeds from the other food offered it. Photo by D. G. Robinson, Jr.

behavior. Also characteristic of desert animals, gerbils conserve internal water quite well. Most of the water they take in comes from the food they eat. In the wild they rarely come into direct contact with drinkable

The Gerbil

water. The gerbil stores its water in layers of fatty cells.

In the wild most gerbil species are nocturnal creatures; that is, they remain in their burrows and sleep

The most intense period of activity usually occurs around midnight, and there may be other weaker activity periods during the remainder of the night and during the day. Like the other gerbil

through most of the day. During the night they prowl for food and nesting material, dig new tunnels and build nests. The Mongolian gerbil is a bit less nocturnal than most. It has periods of activity that last a few hours at a time and are separated by a few hours of rest.

Above: *Like most rodents, gerbils are nocturnal, but they also have periods of activity during the daytime. Domestic gerbils actually may be awake and playing any hour of the day or night.*

Above: *Gerbils love toys. The only requirements are that the material be non-toxic (gerbils will at least sample anything put in their pen) and relatively sturdy to resist their chewing. Gerbils are probably color-blind, but bright colors help accentuate the subdued colors of most gerbils. Photo by M. Gilroy.*

The Gerbil

species, the Mongolian gerbil does not usually come out of its burrow during the hot parts of the day. This nocturnal tendency is one of nature's ways of helping gerbils and other desert animals conserve water. The Mongolian gerbil's and serves as another means of spending as little time as possible on the hot desert sand. The long tail helps the gerbil balance itself during these leaps. Some gerbils can even hop sideways. Their deftness at leaping instantly in

activity cycles are not very different in captivity, even though the intense desert sun is usually missing.

Rather than running as the principal means of locomotion as do true rats, gerbils often tend to hop or jump from place to place. Their leaping behavior is made possible by their large, strong hindlimbs

Above: The well-developed hind legs of the gerbil allow it to both hop and stand up when balanced by the long tail. The amazing ability of the gerbil to seemingly hop in two directions at once never fails to amaze. Photo by S. A. Thompson.

almost any direction except backwards and their ability to leap at least a few feet per jump (by even the poorest jumpers) enable gerbils to survive the perils of predation by their principal enemies, predatory birds and snakes. According to some field reports, the Indian gerbil has come to be known as the antelope rat because of its ability to span a horizontal distance of almost 15 feet in a single leap. The gerbil's jumping ability also comes in quite handy as a means of escaping from or attacking rival gerbils within the colony or immigrant gerbils from other colonies during territorial disputes.

Gerbils are talented burrowers, sometimes forming an intricate network of underground tunnels with special "rooms" for nesting or for storing food. In addition to aiding the gerbil in making its enormous leaps, the large and powerful hindlegs and hindfeet also aid the gerbil in scooping out its burrows. The gerbil digs the soft soil out with the short but strong front claws and then kicks it away with the larger hindfeet. Gerbil burrows usually have numerous exits, making many

Above: *If you don't cover the cage, this is what you will see just before your gerbil goes over the wall. Don't be mislead by their small size—gerbils, even young ones, can jump great distances.*

The Gerbil

escape routes available when a predator invades the burrow. The burrows are most often located near clumps of vegetation where roots aid in holding the soft soil together. This ensures that the tunnels won't collapse under families in warning against predators and sharing some of the food caches; thus gerbils tend to be colonial animals.

Gerbils are not known to stray very far from their burrows, even when they are on forays

ordinary circumstances. The burrows of a number of gerbils are usually located quite close together, and sometimes they interconnect with one another. While each gerbil family maintains its own burrow, there sometimes exists cooperation between

Above: *Gerbils are tunnelling animals used to tight conditions, so when you hold them firmly in your hand they calm down. A firm but not squeezing grip reminds them of home. Photo by K. McGarry.*

for food. Field reports indicate that gerbils rarely wander more than 50 feet from their burrows. This was determined by a researcher who followed their tracks in the snow on a Mongolian desert. Gerbils residing in the

The gerbil's territorial behavior and colonial nature seem to be mediated by chemical means. Both sexes of Mongolian gerbils and most other gerbil species have a scent gland located on the abdomen. The gland

Above: *Gerbils will use any old can as a play burrow. Make sure there are no sharp edges. Photo by K. McGarry.*

northern deserts don't really hibernate *per se* during the winter, but they do become less active and rely more heavily upon the food they have stored in or near their burrows. During this time many of the entrances to the burrows are plugged up, apparently as a means of conserving heat.

contains an oily behavior-mediating substance known as a pheromone (most animals produce one or more types of pheromones that mediate a variety of behaviors). By rubbing their abdomens (hence the scent gland) over objects and over one another, gerbils mark

The Gerbil

their territory and each other. This marking enables the gerbil to distinguish its own territory from other nearby gerbil territories when returning, for instance, from a food foray; it also helps members of the colony identify one another. The individual gerbils of the same species.

One interesting observation I made among my own laboratory populations of gerbils was that in spite of the apparent use of the scent gland as a means of individual

individual marking also enables gerbils to recognize usually unwelcome visitors from neighboring colonies. In all probability, the scent gland plays a significant role in mate identification and in identification of the offspring, especially in view of the fact that research has shown that there are chemical differences between the scent substances of

Above: *This homemade wooden cage will not withstand a gerbil's teeth for very long. Gerbils are among nature's supreme gnawers. Photo by P. Bartley.*

identification, my gerbils occasionally cooperated in looking after each other's pups. On more than one occasion I saw a gerbil (male or female) bring a straggling pup of another gerbil back to its own mother. It is not known whether such

Above: *Although gerbils are usually very tame animals, they will bite if you accidentally pinch them. This gerbil is not being held securely enough. Photo by P. Bartley.*

cooperative behavior occurs in wild populations of gerbils.

Gnawing is another form of behavior frequently observed in wild and domesticated gerbils. The gerbil has grooved incisor teeth that grow constantly. While gnawing serves a practical function in the cutting down of plants for food and nesting material and in the shelling of seeds, without the gnawing habit the gerbil's incisor teeth would grow so long that they would become nonfunctional. This means that the

The Gerbil

gerbil would not be able to eat and would therefore dehydrate rather rapidly, since in the wild its primary source of water is in its food. With nonfunctional incisors it would not be able to prepare nesting material either. The gnawing habit is the main reason that care must be taken in selecting a cage that the animals cannot chew apart.

Scratching is another habit of wild and domesticated gerbils. Like their incisors, their claws grow continuously. Gerbils rapidly claw with the front feet against any

Above: Although the gerbils cannot jump out of this high cage, a cover is still essential to keep other animals from jumping in. Some gerbils become very nervous when cats or dogs are present. Photo by P. Bartley.

hard surface that is available. The scratching keeps the claws reasonably short. Claws that are too long would make it difficult for the gerbil to handle its food in the squirrel-like fashion that it does. There may be other functions to the gerbil's scratching behavior, but if there are, they certainly are not obvious and have not been postulated by any other observers of gerbil behavior. The back claws are presumably kept short enough by the gerbil's usual activities; scratching with the back claws as an isolated behavior without necessarily digging or performing any other function, to the best of my knowledge, has not been observed.

Grooming is a behavior carried out by many vertebrates and also by some invertebrates such as shrimp. Gerbils are no exception. Using the teeth, tongue and sometimes even the claws, gerbils groom themselves. It is not uncommon to see

Below: *Mother gerbils are able to recognize the scent of their own pups, allowing them to return stragglers to the nest with ease. Photo by D. G. Robinson, Jr.*

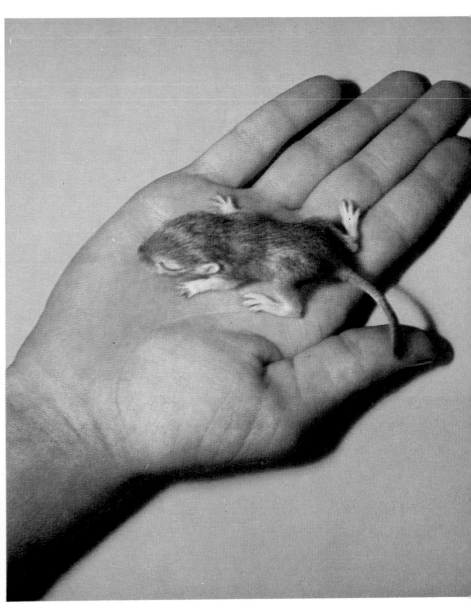

Above: *At two weeks of age this little gerbil looks much like its parents, but it is still not old enough to leave the nest. Photo by D. G. Robinson, Jr.*

Facing page: *Although gerbils are vegetarians, they will investigate small insects and occasionally add them to their diet. Photo of* Taterillus.

gerbils kept in captivity grooming each other. It is reasonable to assume that this activity is performed in the wild, too. If it does occur in the wild, it would most likely occur down in the burrows, so the probability of this behavior being observed in the wild is not very great.

Gerbils are mostly vegetarian in their feeding habits. They subsist on roots, stalks, leaves, flowers and seeds of the plants that are found in their desert habitats. Many of those plants are succulents which provide the gerbil with all the moisture it needs. Gerbils store seeds and other less perishable plant parts in their burrows or under rocks located near their burrows. One species, the great gerbil (*Rhombomys* sp.), is known to store as much as 130 pounds of food in a special chamber in its burrow. Stored food

Above: *Even if an over-
abundance of food is available,
gerbils will still store some of it
away for a rainy day. The natural
instinct to store food for
hibernation is never overcome,
even if hibernation never
occurs. Photo by R. Hanson.*

serves as the bulk of the gerbil's winter food supply. That food storage is an instinctive behavior in gerbils is suggested by the fact that in my laboratory, where more than adequate amounts of food were supplied to my gerbils every day, the animals took food into their burrows and subsequently consumed it days or weeks later. Food storage as an instinctive behavior in many other kinds of animals, including other rodents, has been well documented in scientific literature.

In the wild, gerbils are seldom carnivorous and rarely cannibalistic, although there are some gerbil species that occasionally feed on insects, eat their own young and raid birds' nests to eat the eggs and baby birds. While Mongolian gerbils are not known to be carnivorous in the wild, when kept in captivity in a stressful environment they will devour their young. On a few occasions I observed mother gerbils in my laboratory neglecting some of their pups, especially those that did not seem to have a normal amount of vigor. Eventually these pups were eaten by the mother or by other members of the colony. Usually, however, dead pups were pushed out of the nests and ignored, eventually being buried by the gerbil's constant digging and tunneling activity.

Thumping is another form of cooperative behavior seen in gerbils. To make the thumping noise the gerbil balances itself with its forelimbs and rapidly and simultaneously pounds both hindfeet against the ground. The thumping sounds like a muted, low-frequency vibration. It can be heard resounding through the intricate tunnel system of the gerbil colony. The

Below: *Under stress, the possibility always exists that the mother gerbil may eat her own young. This is not rare when the litter is very young, but it becomes less common as the babies grow larger. Photo by M. Gilroy.*

The Gerbil

thumping gerbil may produce the noise while in its burrow or outside the burrow (but in the immediate vicinity of an opening).

One of the functions of thumping seems to be as a warning system to tell other members of the colony of impending There is some controversy in the literature as to the purpose of the thumping. Some authors claim that thumping is not a signal at all, although they do not postulate an alternative explanation. During the period of time that I

danger from a nearby predator. Another purpose seems to be to inform the members of the colony that there is a "stranger" in the vicinity, said stranger being a gerbil from another colony. Thumping seems to trigger the appropriate flight or fight response in all the members of the colony.

Above: *A strange gerbil visiting the home of another gerbil will usually draw a thumping response, even if there is no obvious danger involved. Photo by M. Gilroy.*

worked with gerbils in my laboratory, I observed thumping on numerous occasions when I attempted to transfer gerbils from one pen to another and also

Above: *This cinnamon gerbil is on the alert. Perhaps one of its cage mates has given a warning thump. Photo by M. Gilroy.*

after I introduced new gerbils to an established colony. On the former occasions the gerbils all took cover following the thumping. Although the

The Gerbil

presence of my hand in the pen may well have been the cause of the gerbils taking flight, my action was not sudden or startling, and the gerbils usually did not run for cover until one gerbil began to thump.

eventually having a scuffle with it.

How the gerbils distinguish a flight thump from a fight thump has not been established. It could be by the frequency of the thumping in each series

On the occasions when a stranger was introduced into the colony, and following subsequent thumping by one gerbil, some members of the colony gathered around the stranger, sniffing it and

Above: *Small naked-sole gerbils, Taterillus, from eastern Africa.*

Facing page: *Gerbils are visually alert animals, as might be guessed from their large eyes. Photo by M. Gilroy.*

of thumps or by the time span between each thumping series. Several seconds of continuous thumping rarely occurs as an entity - the thumping vibration is usually repeated a few times with a few seconds between each series. On the other hand, perhaps the difference between the flight thump and the fight thump lies in the loudness of the thumping. Perhaps there are also other sensory factors such as olfaction involved. It is indeed an interesting question and one that could possibly be answered, at least as far as laboratory populations are concerned, in an academic study by someone who has the necessary funds and time.

Gerbils have also been observed thumping during individual rival fights over territory or a mate. Sometimes a few series of rapid thumps seem to frighten off a challenger, but a more aggressive challenger may return the thumps. It seems to be the

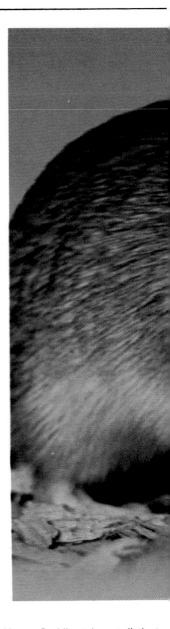

Above: *Gerbils stake out distinct territories that are guarded to some extent. In domestic situations the territories may not be obvious except during mating.*

location of the thumping battles rather than the forcefulness of the thumping that determines who the winner of the battle will be. As with most territorial animals, the deeper into the defender's territory a duel occurs, the less likely it is that the

The Gerbil

Above: *The litter in a gerbil's territory will soon take on the gerbil's own distinctive scent that is recognized by other animals in the cage. Photo by G. Axelrod.*

Mongolian gerbils have one of the most well-developed thermoregulation systems known among the various gerbil species studied. This species can tolerate for prolonged periods of time temperatures as high as 100°F. as well as temperatures below freezing. Such a wide tolerance is not lost in captivity, provided the temperature changes are not brought about too suddenly. Although this wide temperature tolerance indicates a very hardy animal, the Mongolian gerbil is no less susceptible to disease brought about by a sudden chill than is any other animal. If the gerbil is plucked out of an 85-degree environment and suddenly placed into a 32-degree environment, it will become ill and probably die as a result.

The gerbil's ability to conserve water, which was mentioned earlier, is one of this animal's most remarkable features. Because of the gerbil's lack of direct water consumption (in

challenger will win.

Thumping possibly serves one other very important purpose for the gerbil. It appears to be an intricate part of mating behavior. During courtship an estrous female usually presents her hindquarters to her mate following his thumping. If the female is not estrous, she does not respond to thumping or any other sexual stimuli.

Above: *In the middle of the belly of the gerbil is a patch of specialized skin with glands that secrete a type of musk. This is the scent gland. When marking a territory, the gerbil rubs its belly along an object to determine a border that will be recognized by other gerbils. Photo by R. Hanson.*

natural situations) and its ability to store water in the cells of fatty tissue, it produces only a drop or two of highly concentrated urine per day. Its feces are produced in the form of hard, odorless pellets. For these reasons, the gerbil's burrows do not very easily become fouled, and for the very same reason the Mongolian gerbil is a very popular pet animal.

Its curiosity is another reason for the gerbil's great popularity

Above: *Because of their innate curiosity, gerbils are attracted to new sounds and sights. For this reason they have come to be known as attentive, active, very friendly pets. Photo by P. Bartley.*

as a pet. The gerbil does not usually run or hide from a new noise. Rather, it is attracted by a new sound and investigates the sound before "deciding" whether or not it means danger. This curious response to sounds that would frighten most other rodents away may be due to the gerbil's keen sense of hearing and its innate talent for swiftly and adroitly jumping out of harm's way when necessary. It

Above: *Although gerbils have only been in captivity on a large scale for under a half century, they have already gone through enough captive generations that mutations are showing up. Among the first color mutations were those involving large areas of white in the body color.*

The gerbil has acute hearing that allows it to detect the approach of enemies from a considerable distance. The upright ears also add to the gerbil's alert appearance. Photo by M. Gilroy.

The dove or pale gray coat of this gerbil would blend very well into the colors of its native plains. Photo by M. Gilroy.

is possible that the gerbil can hear the enemy's approach from a greater distance than can less curious rodents.

While the Mongolian desert habitats from which the Mongolian gerbil comes are not exactly poor in faunal diversity, this diversity is not overly rich either. There aren't a whole lot of animals that can tolerate the harsh extremes of this environment, hence the number of the gerbil's natural enemies is not as great as it might be if the gerbil lived in a temperate or tropical forest. All of this is, of course, only conjecture, but it is conjecture based upon certain undeniable physiological and ecological information.

For whatever reason it is that gerbils are so curious, it is a fact that their curious nature has helped a great deal in establishing them as a common pet in the western world. Because they are so easily tamed, handled and trained,

Few small animals can look as alert as can a gerbil. The upright posture, erect ears, large eyes, and twitching nose all add to the effect. Photo by M. Gilroy.

The Gerbil

Mongolian gerbils are also popular research animals for behavioral research. For example, the United States Federal Aviation Agency has invested some money in a research program aimed at training gerbils to sniff out bombs at airports. Gerbils may actually turn out to be more useful than hound dogs for this purpose - their sense of smell may be almost as keen and they are certainly a lot easier to care for than are most dogs.

Gerbils are also finding a place for themselves in biomedical research. One example is the recent finding by a group of Swiss scientists in Basel that gerbils (and the Mongolian gerbil in particular) make excellent laboratory models for studying bilharziasis, a human disease also known as schistosomiasis. This debilitating disease affects nearly 300 million people in Latin America, Africa, the Middle East and the Far East. The parasitic worm that causes the disease is carried by certain snails, and it is usually a different species of snail in each part of the world that the disease occurs. One very severe form of the disease, which destroys the urinary tract and may be linked to bladder cancer, occurs in Madagascar. Another variety that leaves its victims badly crippled occurs in Asia. It was reportd by David A. Ehrlich in a 1978 number of the *Ciba-Geigy Journal* that the ease with which the Mongolian gerbil can be infected with many forms of the disease and the ease with which the disease can be maintained in these gerbils have significantly boosted bilharziasis research. The Mongolian gerbil may well turn out to be the ideal research animal of the future.

Facing page: Several of the available color mutations of gerbils first turned up in laboratory animals being used for medical experiments. Photo by M. Gilroy.

Above: *Your local pet shop will have a wide array of gerbil foods and treats, plus all the things you need to keep your gerbil healthy. Photo by Dr. Herbert R. Axelrod.*

Feeding

To breed gerbils successfully, which means having normal, healthy offspring, it is important that they be properly fed and nourished. Not only must they get enough food, but they must get enough of the right kinds of foods. This is no startling revelation, for it is true of any organism including yourself. However, it is easy to make mistakes in feeding pets. For example, many people find it fascinating to watch a gerbil sit up on its haunches and manipulate a sunflower seed with its teeth and front claws - gerbils shell the seeds with much less effort than we humans do. The eventual result of this fascination is often that the gerbil rarely receives anything to eat but sunflower seeds. While the seeds contain plenty of nutrition, they also contain more fat and carbohydrate than many other foods gerbils eat. Furthermore, sunflower seeds don't contain all the proteins, minerals and vitamins that gerbils need - no one type of food does. On an overly rich diet consisting mostly of sunflower seeds, gerbils soon become obese and lethargic, and their fur becomes rough and dull. Sooner or later this "hot" or rich diet causes digestive disorders which eventually cause

Above: *Gerbils will enjoy the addition of small amounts of fresh vegetables to their diet. Be careful of spoilage, however.*

the appetite to wane. This weakens the animals and makes them much more susceptible to a variety of diseases. These complications also affect reproduction, slowing it down or even bringing it to an abrupt halt. Offspring fed on milk from a malnourished mother lack normal vigor. In short, a fat, malnourished gerbil is an unhealthy gerbil.

Protein is an essential ingredient of any animal diet. Proteins are the basic building blocks of all living tissue. There are millions of different

Above: *To live to a healthy old age (for a gerbil) the animal must get a balanced diet that will fill all the requirements for gerbil nutrition. Too much of any one group of nutrients, such as carbohydrates, could lead to health problems and a shortened life. Foods bought in pet stores are usually well balanced. Photo by M. Gilroy.*

kinds of proteins, and they are all basically made of about 20 amino acids linked together in varying sequences of differing lengths and conformations. Plants synthesize their own amino acids from raw materials, but animals do not. In order to build the proteins their cells are genetically coded for, animals must get the amino acids from an outside source, namely their food. When animals eat proteins their digestive systems break those proteins down into their basic amino acids, which are then distributed to all the cells in the body via the circulatory system. When the genetic code in a cell calls for a particular amino acid, it must be available in order for the correct protein to be built. Feeding your gerbils a high-protein diet does not necessarily mean they will have all the amino acids they need— it merely means they will have a lot of some of them. The exact proportion of each amino acid needed is not known. Therefore, the only way to ensure that your gerbils will have all the amino acids they need is to see to it that they eat a wide variety of proteins that they can only get by eating a wide variety of foods.

Variety, then, is the examples, growth hormones will be produced in sufficient quantity to ensure proper growth, and sexual and reproductive hormones will be produced in the right quantity and at the right time to ensure good reproduction. A well-

key to a healthful diet, not only for the correct balance of amino acids but also for the correct balance of all other nutrients - the fats, the carbohydrates, the minerals, the vitamins and the fiber. A well-balanced diet helps every one of the gerbil's internal systems function properly. As

Above: *Although most gerbils go absolutely wild over sunflower seeds and wil eat them as fast as they are offered, these seeds are too rich in carbohydrates to be given as more than a snack or treat. Obese gerbils are relatively inactive and have shorter lives than do healthy gerbils. Photo by D. G. Robinson, Jr.*

nourished female gerbil will produce the right balance of substances in her milk, and this will ensure that her pups get a good start in life.

The proper combination of nutrients in the diet is as important as the variety of each nutrient. For example, fats and carbohydrates provide the gerbil with the necessary fuel for breaking down or metabolizing the protein intake and for the construction of new proteins from raw amino acids. Without adequate fats and carbohydrates, a good portion of the protein intake is wasted or, in other words, not utilized efficiently - carbohydrates and some fats have a protein-sparing (saving) effect. Fats and carbohydrates also provide energy for every other body function. Without an adequate energy input, the hormone and nervous systems cannot work together properly. Correct breeding behavior and every other kind of behavior depend

Above: *A nicely balanced meal for a group of gerbils. Notice that the high-fat and high-carbohydrate seeds such as sunflower seeds are balanced off with kibble and with other grains. Photo by M. Gilroy.*

heavily upon the gerbil's having adequate energy.

Minerals, and a variety of them, are necessary for the maintenance of a correct electrolytic balance and for many other functions. Without the right amounts of sodium and potassium, for instance, the circulatory system to carry vital oxygen to every cell in the body. Phosphorus is an essential mineral for metabolism. Iodine also plays an important role in metabolism and in growth via the thyroid gland.

A number of different vitamins must also be

resultant incorrect electrolytic balance causes neural disorders that can affect nearly everything the gerbil does. Calcium is necessary for the proper building of bones and teeth and is an essential requirement for successful pregnancies and lactation (milk production). Adequate amounts of iron enable

Above: *Minerals of various types are also important in the diet of the healthy gerbil, but they are usually present in the correct amounts and proportions in the balanced diet from the pet store. Photo by S. A. Thompson.*

incorporated into the gerbil's diet in order to prevent a whole host of deficiency diseases. A shortage of vitamin D, calcium and phosphorus will impair metabolism; bone and tooth deformities may occur. Scurvy can result from inadequate vitamin C. There is much evidence that vitamin C is instrumental in helping animals build resistance to many bacterial and viral diseases. Vitamin A, derived largely from carotenoids (yellow vegetable matter) has a direct effect on growth and disease resistance as well as reproduction, the latter especially in

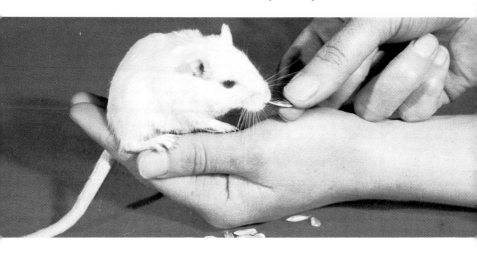

Above: *One of the easiest tricks to teach a gerbil is eating out of your hand. Most gerbils will do anything for a sunflower seed. Anyway, gerbils are not exactly shy animals once they get to know you. Photo by R. Hanson.*

females. Adequate vitamin E is necessary for reproduction, especially in males. A severe vitamin E shortage can cause irreversible sterility. There are many other vitamin and mineral complexes that play essential roles in all of the gerbil's life functions.

Finally, the gerbil

must have adequate fiber and other roughage in the diet. Roughage helps keep food moving through the digestive tract. Without an adequate amount, severe digestive disorders will result. Even though every other nutrient may be present in the diet and in the correct amounts, little of it will find its way into

Now that gerbils have come into prominence as pets, there are commercially packaged food mixes labeled as gerbil food. In some cases these mixes are identical with those packaged as hamster food. There is nothing wrong with this, however, because the nutritional requirements of gerbils

the gerbil's various systems without enough roughage to carry it through the alimentary canal.

Following are some dietary suggestions that will ensure an adequate variety of all the essential nutrients a gerbil requires for good growth and reproduction.

Above: *The newer colored gerbils, such as the ivory and the cinnamon white spot shown here, are from lines that have been in captivity for generations, so they are well adjusted to the diets of seeds and pellets that are sold in pet shops and fed to domesticated animals. Photo by M. Gilroy.*

Above: *Because gerbils feed largely on dry seeds and pellets, their basic diet is just about the same as that of hamsters, and packaged food suitable for one animal can be fed to the other without harm. Rabbits and guinea pigs have different requirements, however, and their food should not be given to gerbils in large amounts. Photo by G. Axelrod.*

and hamsters are just about the same. These packages contain an assortment of grains such as wheat, oats, barley and corn (cracked or whole-kernel) as well as peanuts, sunflower seeds, pumpkin seeds, other small seeds, egg flakes (made from egg yolk, tapioca flour and cornstarch), vegetable flakes (made from parsley, spinach, carrots and other vegetables) and rabbit pellets. Such a mix usually contains all of the nutrient materials needed by gerbils and can form the mainstay of the gerbil diet most of the time. If, however, you intend to raise gerbils in any great number and for long periods of time, these mixes can be a bit expensive. There are some cases, then, when it pays to make your own mix or to feed gerbils different types of foods on a rotating schedule. Furthermore, sometimes for unknown reasons gerbils go into periods of feeding lethargy; feeding them one particular type of food for a while, one they haven't been getting much of before, can often solve the problem. However, once they begin to eat with renewed gusto, other foods should be worked into the diet.

Rabbit pellets are very small, cylinder-shaped chunks of food that are high in green vegetable matter as well as other nutrients. These pellets are relatively inexpensive. Some gerbils seem to favor them quite

strongly, while others do not.

Rat pellets are much larger than rabbit pellets, and their greens content is a little lower. These cylindrical pellets are about an inch long and a half-inch thick. Gerbils seem to enjoy gnawing on these large pellets, which are highly nutritious. If fed often enough, rat pellets provide gerbils with sufficient gnawing exercise to keep the long incisor teeth adequately shortened and sharp.

Monkey pellets, while high in many of the right nutrients for gerbils, are much softer than rat or rabbit pellets. This is due to their higher

Facing page: *This black gerbil is in one of his favorite positions, standing up and holding food in his front feet. Many gerbils like to gnaw on pellets of food for long periods of time. When feeding pellets, remember that gerbils will store some, so they must not be subject to fungus. Photo by M. Gilroy.*

YES! Please enter my subscription to *Tropical Fish Hobbyist*. I enclose payment for the length I've selected. U.S. funds only.

☐ 1 year—$30.00   ☐ 2 years—$55.00   ☐ 3 years —$75.00   ☐ 5 years—$120.00
12 BIG ISSUES   24 ISSUES   36 ISSUES   60 ISSUES

Canada, add $11.00 per year; Foreign add $16.00 per year. Please allow 4-6 weeks for your subscription to start.

Prices subject to change without notice.

☐ SAMPLE ISSUE—$3.50 ☐ LIFETIME MEMBERSHIP $495.00 (maximum 30 years)

☐ GIFT SUBSCRIPTION. Please send a card announcing this gift. I would like the card to read:

SEND TO:

Name _____

Street _____ Apt. No. _____

City _____ State _____ Zip _____

CHARGE my: ☐ VISA ☐ MASTER CHARGE ☐ PAYMENT ENCLOSED

|_|_|_|_|_|_|_|_|_|_|_|_|_|_|_|_| (Minimum order charge $15)
Card Number

Cardholder's Name (if different from "Send to:") _____

Cardholder's Address (if different from "Send to:") _____

Cardholder's Signature

moisture content as well as some of their specific ingredients. They do not provide gerbils with adequate gnawing exercise, and they do not keep as well in storage as do rat and rabbit pellets.

Cracked or whole-kernel dried corn can be purchased cheaply. This provides the gerbil with high amounts of carbohydrates and carotenoids, the latter of which are a class of proteins that help

Above: *If you feel your gerbil may not be getting a perfectly balanced diet, you can always give it vitamin supplements. Several brands of water-soluble vitamins are available at your dealer's. However, remember that vitamins only add to a diet, they cannot counteract the faults in a poor diet. Photo by G. Axelrod.*

provide the gerbil with a good rich coat color.

Grains such as barley, oats and wheat, as well as wheat germ, can be purchased in separate packages and offered to the gerbil individually, as a grain mix or mixed with other foods.

Sunflower seeds as a food for gerbils fall into a class all by themselves, for they seem to be one of the gerbil's favorite foods. As mentioned earlier, they are very rich in fats and carbohydrates and therefore should not be fed in excessive quantities. Sunflower seeds can be fed to a lactating female in somewhat greater quantities than normal, for they do seem to boost milk production. However, once the young are weaned the use of sunflower seeds should be reduced. Aside from their food value, sunflower seeds have another great value to gerbils: the husks of sunflower seeds are used as bedding and nesting material. I found it pure fascination to watch newly weaned or nearly weaned gerbils learn to husk sunflower seeds. On the first attempt it usually takes the juvenile gerbil a minute or longer to shell the seed. With each new attempt the task becomes easier and easier. Finally, often after only a half-dozen attempts, the young gerbil masters the task and can do it in only a few seconds.

Peanuts in the shell can be given to gerbils. It doesn't take them very long to learn how to get the "reward" in the middle, and the shells are also quite useful as nesting material.

Prepackaged mixtures of just seeds are commercially available and are usually sold for feeding birds such as finches or canaries. These seed mixtures are readily eaten by gerbils, especially newly weaned pups. Some of the seeds contained in these mixtures are the same kinds that are used in commercially packaged gerbil food mixes.

Alfalfa is sold in small

packages by pet shops, mainly for use with rabbits and guinea pigs. Gerbils will, however, eat small amounts of alfalfa, although they may have more of a tendency to use it as a nesting material.

For occasional dietary variety, certain types of hard dog biscuits can be given to gerbils. Some of these are especially high in calcium and phosphorus and can be as useful in a gerbil's diet as they are in a dog's diet for helping the animals maintain healthy bones, teeth and claws as well as all the other bodily functions served by these minerals. In addition, like rat pellets, hard dog biscuits provide the gerbil with gnawing material for tooth maintenance.

Gerbil treats are available commercially. They are nutritious and serve as good gnawing material, but like any specialty food, their excessive use will cause a dietary imbalance. In addition, they are rather expensive. They should be used, as their name

Above: *For these three-week-old babies to grow into healthy adults, they should be given a balanced diet, acceptable snacks and treats, clean cage conditions, and proper temperature and lighting. Gerbils are easy to raise with basic care. Photo by M. Gilroy.*

implies, only as treats.

While hard pelleted foods and a variety of seeds can and should be the mainstay of the gerbil's diet, fresh vegetables should also be included. Pelleted foods and seeds do contain most of the needed nutrient materials, but they generally lack the necessary amounts of some of the essential vitamins and minerals. Most important, however, is the fact that these foods do not contain nearly enough water to satisfy the gerbil's needs. In fact, remembering our earlier discussion on the gerbil's natural sources of water, it is from live vegetable matter that wild gerbils derive nearly all of their water intake. If fresh vegetables are used judiciously in the gerbil's diet, it is not necessary to provide drinking water at all.

There are two good sources of vegetables for gerbils. One is, of course, the supermarket or produce store. Although this can be an expensive source of food, the variety of vegetables found in the supermarket is unquestionably a plus in favor of their use. Lettuce, cabbage, kale, broccoli, celery and almost any other kind of green vegetable will provide gerbils not only with all the water they need, but also with a variety of necessary vitamins such as vitamin A, a great part of the vitamin B complex and vitamin C. Root vegetables such as carrots, turnips and beets are also readily eaten by gerbils, and they too provide many essential vitamins. Fresh vegetables are also a good source of essential minerals such as calcium, potassium, phosphorus, iron, zinc

Facing page: *The gleam in the eyes of this gerbil shows that it is healthy. Although not one of the new colors, the standard agouti pattern is still preferred by many gerbil owners.*

Feeding

and others as well as trace minerals such as manganese and magnesium to mention only a few. Finally, fresh vegetables provide gerbils with much of the cellulose (roughage) they require for proper digestion.

A much less expensive way to provide gerbils with fresh vegetable matter is to use certain weeds that are commonly found growing in lawns, empty lots, fields and forests. These plants are free for the taking. Useful weeds are dandelions, chickweed, clovers and grasses. One important precaution in choosing weeds is to make sure the areas were not recently sprayed with insecticides or herbicides. These chemicals, if present in any sizable quantity, can make gerbils quite ill and can even kill them. If you are not sure about the presence of these compounds in the area you've chosen to harvest weeds from, it is best not to use these plants.

Whether store-bought vegetables or wild plants, they should be rinsed thoroughly before feeding them to your gerbils. Washing will rid the vegetables of dirt, bacteria from domesticated or wild animal excreta and harmful insects.

Fresh vegetables should not be fed in excess to gerbils, for the result will be gastro-intestinal upsets and diarrhea. Aside from the direct harm of the upset itself, abnormally wet excreta can provide a breeding ground for harmful bacteria and insects. This can result in other diseases in the gerbils. If you are in doubt as to how much vegetable matter to use, then it is best to use very little and provide your gerbils instead with water containing a few drops of vitamin supplements that are specially compounded

Facing page: *Pregnant gerbils are great hoarders of food. Be sure that they do not try to save pieces of carrot or lettuce that could spoil. Photo by M. Gilroy.*

Above: *This is not a snack! Although sunflower seeds may be loved by gerbils, they should not be fed as a dominant part of the meal. Experiment with your gerbil's diet to find healthy foods that will give the gerbil both pleasure and the proper balance of nutrients. If your gerbil develops a liking for roasted peanuts, a few now and then will not hurt it. The same goes for many types of vegetables and fruits that are liked by some animals and disliked by others. Experiment.*

for use with gerbils, hamsters and other small mammals. A few small pieces of fresh vegetable matter twice a week are usually sufficient for most gerbils as long as supplementary water is available when the animals want it. This small amount of vegetable matter is essential in the long run to the gerbil's well-being and definitely should not be dispensed with entirely. A little bit of experience and perhaps a few minor but reversible errors will tell you exactly how much vegetable matter to feed your gerbils. Don't be afraid to experiment with your gerbil's diet, but while experimenting use common sense and your errors will all be minor ones.

If you are using a variety of foods rather than a prepackaged mixture of foods, it is helpful and perhaps even necessary to prepare a written feeding schedule. This ensures that the various foods are rotated into the diet at regular intervals. In the long run this will prevent deficiency-caused diseases and will promote good growth and excellent reproduction.

Proper food storage is vital to the health of your gerbils. Dry foods such as pellets and seeds must be kept dry to prevent spoilage and must be kept in containers that are vermin-proof. There is no quicker way to draw germ-laden cockroaches, flies, rats and mice into your house than to leave pet food exposed. Soft foods and vegetables (including weeds) should be stored in the refrigerator. Pelleted foods and seeds can be stored there, too, but can be stored more easily in tightly sealed bins, in new unused trash cans with tight-fitting lids or in cleaned-out coffee cans with plastic lids. If you suspect that there has been some vermin in the gerbil's food or that the food is otherwise spoiled, it is best not to take any chances with

Feeding

it - discard it and buy fresh food. Gerbils are just as sensitive to disease and gastrointestinal upsets from spoiled foods as are humans, so if you are serious about breeding and raising gerbils, be very careful with food storage.

There are several acceptable ways to present food to gerbils, but scattering food about the cage bottom is not one of them. It's bad enough that the gerbils themselves sooner or later make a mess of the cage by scattering food everywhere. You don't need to accelerate the process by doing it for them. Once the gerbils have made a nest, they will carry food to the nest where it will be stored. In the process a lot of it will be scattered about, and some food is bound to drop into damp areas where water

has been spilled or the gerbils have urinated. Since this food will spoil, it should be removed from the cage as soon as possible.

Introduce food by placing it in a shallow dish or plate, preferably one made of a heavy ceramic material so the gerbils won't be able to drag it around or turn it over. If commercial or laboratory breeding cages are used, the

Above: *The posture and behavior of your gerbil can indicate if it is ill. One of the most common illnesses is gastrointestinal upset from spoiled stored food. Photo by S.A. Thompson.*

Facing page: *Unlike hamsters, a gerbil does not run around with its cheek pouches filled with food. In fact, it is difficult to see the cheek pouches in gerbils engaged in everyday activities such as grooming. Photo by M. Gilroy.*

cage cover usually contains a built-in food hopper which allows the animals to remove food as they want it.

Where watering is concerned, until you've had a lot of experience with gerbils it is best to provide the gerbils with fresh vegetables only two times a week and make water constantly available to them. Water can be placed in a dish, but that is very messy at best. The best way to

provide water for gerbils is to use a water bottle outfitted with a stopper and a stainless steel drinking tube. The watering bottle hooks onto the cage or fits into a special compartment in the cage top in such a position that the gerbils can drink water as they need it without spilling it all over the cage. The water in the bottle should be replaced several times a week, and liquid vitamin supplements can be added to the water in the bottle.

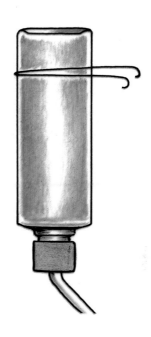

Facing page: *A cinnamon and a dove gerbil in the full glow of health. Photo by M. Gilroy.*

Above: *A water bottle with a drinking tube.* Below: *Cage dividers can be used to keep males and females apart before and after mating.*

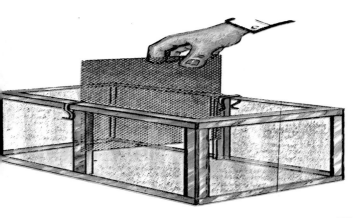

Gerbils and their young. Photo by M. Gilroy.

Housing

Above: *This gorgeous white (actually albino—note the red eye) gerbil is displayed in a photographer's background. In its cage the litter must be kept very clean so as not to discolor its fur.· Photo by M. Gilroy.*

The choice of housing for gerbils is very broad, for they are very adaptable animals. I kept my gerbils in very large aquaria (30- to 50-gallon capacity) filled with clay soil to a depth of about 12 inches. Some large rocks were buried in the soil to add support to the gerbils' burrows. Wire cage covers were used over the tops of the tanks. In this setup it is important that the soil not be allowed to become exceedingly dry, otherwise enormous amounts of dust would be scattered about and the burrows would easily collapse. This is taken care of by using a garden sprinkling can to moisten the habitat. A small amount of water, just enough to replace that lost to evaporation, is gently sprinkled all over the habitat daily.

Aquaria of 30- to 50-gallon capacity are necessary in order to have enough soil for the gerbils to burrow into and at the same time have at least six inches of space between the

Above: *A gerbil at play in discarded boxes with "crawl spaces."* Below: *A minimal cage setup for a pair of gerbils. Open wire cages are not the best.*

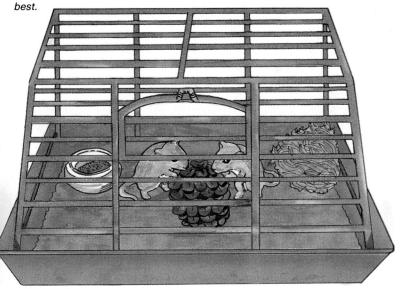

soil surface and the cage cover. This gives the gerbils room to stand during feeding, drinking, courting and any other activities carried out on the surface of the habitat. Obviously the cover must be very secure to prevent the gerbils from forcing it open because they are so close to the top.

There are several advantages to this type of gerbil housing. The greatest is the space it gives the animals. This encourages breeding and enables at least two generations (parents and first generation offspring) to be raised to maturity and live together as a colony. It is by far the cleanest kind of gerbil housing, for there is no urine or water-soaked litter to change. Droppings and urine-soaked soil tend to get scattered about and buried where they are at least partially degraded by natural biological processes. (I found it not necessary to change these habitats more often than twice a year.) This kind of habitat allows the gerbil-keeper with a more academic

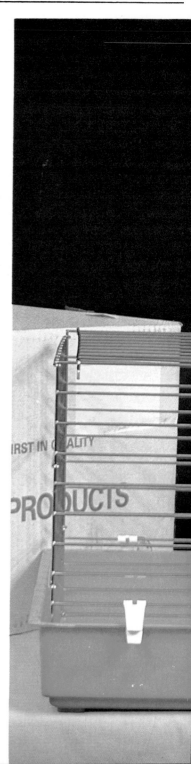

Facing page: *The major problem with this type of cage when used for gerbils is that the young animals can crawl right out between the bars. Cats can also reach in with ease.*

interest in the animals to observe their burrowing behavior, since the burrows are very often made right against the glass of the aquarium.

One of the disadvantages of this kind of habitat is that it is not easy to remove gerbils from it without intentionally collapsing their tunnels in order to grab them - there is always the possibility that suckling pups in a subterranean nest will get buried alive. Another disadvantage is that you will not always know when a gerbil has died, and this could foul the habitat. Of course, if the habitat is large enough, this will not be a factor. Because of the difficulty of handling the animals in this kind of setup, it should not be used if large-scale reproduction is your reason for keeping gerbils.

Facing page: *The ultimate gerbil toy: a cardboard tube. This will provide hours of fun until the whole thing is gnawed to dust. Be sure that any excess glue on the tube is safe or removed. Photo by M. Gilroy.*

More conventional housing for gerbils consists of an aquarium of adequate size, a simple metal cage or a deep plastic pan covered with a wire or screen top. The top usually contains depressions or some sort of accommodations for food and for a water bottle. Because of the gerbil's use of litter as nesting material, it is necessary that the chosen cage not have a wire bottom as is often used for rats and rabbits. The cage should have a solid bottom.

As far as cage size is concerned, the accommodations should be at least six inches deep to allow the gerbils to feed and drink in an upright position. A floor area of six inches by eight inches is adequate for one gerbil, although more room will mean less cleaning and better breeding results. A 10-gallon aquarium (20 inches long by 10 inches wide) or a metal cage about the same size is just about right for four or five adult gerbils or an adult pair and one

Above: *Notice the closer spacing of the wires in this cage. Remember that the cage is both to keep the gerbils in and to keep out enemies. Photo by Dr. Herbert R. Axelrod.*

litter of pups, at least until the pups are young adults (two months of age).

The cage should be kept in a dry, draft-free location. While gerbils have a high tolerance for a wide range of temperatures, sudden temperature changes and cold drafts will cause them to have colds and other respiratory ailments.

Bedding material will be needed in the gerbil cage. Bedding serves two purposes. First, it absorbs the little bit of urine that gerbils produce, thus helping keep the cage cleaner. Secondly, the gerbils use the bedding as a nesting material, chewing it into strands and bits and piling it up in a chosen corner of the cage. The best bedding material is wood shavings. Several different kinds are packaged commercially. There are cedar shavings that have a natural strong odor that helps conceal the sometimes offensive odors of small pets. This and other deodorizing wood shavings are not really necessary for gerbils because, as mentioned earlier, they produce very little urine and their stool takes the form of hard, odorless pellets. However, unless you wish to get out the old jack plane and shave some wood yourself, you'll likely have to buy deodorant shavings, for that is usually all that is available in small quantities. That's okay, however, because the deodorant bedding will not harm the gerbils. Also available are chlorophyll-scented and lemon-scented shavings. If you wish to buy large sacks of shavings, plain shavings are available from animal feed specialty stores or farm supply stores.

A one-inch layer of shavings on the cage

Below: *All the items you need to house your gerbil safely and healthily are available at your local pet shop. There you will also find the helpful advice you may need from time to time. Photo by G. Axelrod.*

Above: *Although it is likely that many or most gerbil cages are provided with hamster exercise wheels, many keepers feel there are dangers involved in having them in a gerbil cage. A gerbil has a long and rather fragile tail, while a hamster has only a stub. If a gerbil gets its tail caught in the wheel, it can suffer serious damage.*

bottom is usually satisfactory. The litter or shavings should be replaced approximately every two weeks in a 10-inch by 20-inch cage containing four gerbils. If it becomes foul-smelling sooner than that, you may be over-feeding and over-watering your gerbils - or the gerbils may be ill.

Improvement of the strain should be one of the primary goals of the gerbil-breeder. Improvement by selection is not a difficult process and does not require advanced knowledge in the field of genetics. It does require having some basic information about elementary hereditary processes, however, and that will be provided here. Improvement by selection takes a keen eye and a keen ability to observe gerbil behavior - both talents are easily developed with a little bit of experience and a lot of plain old common sense.

In order to develop a strain of gerbils worthy of your efforts to improve them, it pays to start out with superior animals in the first place. Buying poor-quality stock because it is cheaper seldom brings satisfactory results - it may take several years of effort just to bring the animals up to the quality of average stock. The chances of making any

The mating of this dove female with an agouti Canadian white spot male has yielded a litter containing blacks as well as young similar to the parents. Photo by M. Gilroy.

significant improvements in a strain of gerbils derived from poor stock are pretty remote.

So what does one look for in purchasing initial breeding stock? To begin with, one should consider only young specimens. Two-month-old gerbils are ideal. They have been on their own for about five weeks and have passed through the more critical infantile stages in which they are most likely to have been affected by any diseases carried in their genes. They have also passed through the period of their lives in which their susceptibility to environmentally caused diseases is highest. If they've made it this far and come through in good health, it's a pretty sure bet that they will make good breeding stock. At the age of two months they are still very adaptable to new conditions. Older gerbils, like any other animal, are more set in their ways and don't adapt as readily to new conditions. At two months of age gerbils

Above: *Albino is a recessive, so to get the young albino gerbil shown here with its mother, the father must have at least carried albino in its genetic makeup.*

are easy enough to sex
that it is not difficult to
select just one pair,
although preselection of
potential mates by the
breeder doesn't always
work. It is recommended
that the breeder start off
with at least four
youngsters (two of each
sex). Once the gerbils
have ''decided'' which
will be whose partner,
the extra pair or the
unpaired gerbils
(however their

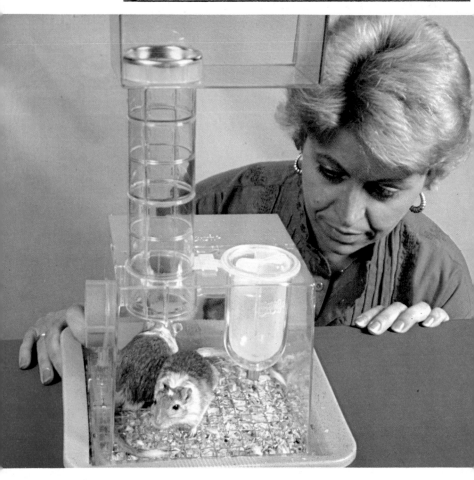

arrangements turn out) can be placed in a separate cage, given away or otherwise disposed of.

Although in fully matured gerbils males tend to be a little larger than females, this is not a reliable means of sexing gerbils raised in captivity, young or old. Conditions under which domesticated gerbils

Above: *Pied gerbils were among the first color mutants bred successfully. Since no two are exactly alike and it is almost impossible to predict the pattern of offspring from even two similar parents, the color has never become popular. Photo by G. Axelrod.*

have been raised play a major role in their size, and rearing methods are not consistent from one breeder to another.

The best way to sex gerbils is to examine their genital areas. This is done by holding them at the base of the tail between your thumb and forefinger and looking at the area just under the tail base. There is nothing especially outstanding to notice in the female's genital area, but the male has a large black, nearly hairless patch in this area. This is the scrotum which protects the reproductive organs. It is quite outstanding and makes the male easy to distinguish from the female. This sexing method must be carried out quickly, as gerbils are not very tolerant of being dangled upside down by the tail. After a few seconds a gerbil will begin to struggle, and this can result in severe injuries to the gerbil as well as to the person handling it. It is imperative that the tail be held as close to the gerbil's rump as

possible and very firmly so that the pressure is on the caudal vertebrae rather than just on the skin covering. Otherwise the tail could be stripped of its skin covering during the animal's struggle to right itself.

The potential breeder gerbil should have clear, shiny black eyes (unless

Above: *Sexing gerbils. In males there are two nearly hairless patches in front of the tail.*

it is a pink-eyed albino). The snout should not be very wet. The fur should be smooth and shiny. The tail of a two-month-old gerbil should be at least three-fourths the length of the body, and it should be perfectly straight, lacking any kinks or nodules. The tail should be uniformly covered with fur from the tip to the base - on

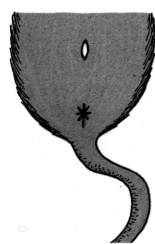

View of rear underside of female gerbil, showing relative closeness of vagina and anus.

View of rear underside of male gerbil, showing relatively large space between scrotum and anus.

the underside as well as on the top. There should be a slight tuft of fur at the tip of the tail. The hindlimbs and forelimbs, including the tops of the feet, should be well covered with fur. The claws should be dark in color and uniform in length. The belly should be uniformly covered (except near the genitals) with fur that is nearly as dense as that on the back and flanks. The ears should be fur-covered on the outside and should be held erect. There should be no sores around the mouth or snout. If you can possibly see into the gerbil's mouth, it should have a uniform pink color (including the tongue).

The gerbil should be alert and active. Don't judge the quality of a gerbil during one of its quiescent periods or you'll not know if it is active and alert until you take it home - and don't disturb its rest to find out! If the gerbil runs scared when you approach the cage there is something wrong, and it should not be purchased. As explained earlier, gerbils are naturally inquisitive animals, and if the gerbils are in good health your appearance should arouse their curiosity, thus drawing them to the site of your approach.

Gerbils with bald spots on the head, back, tail or feet are either suffering from hereditary defects or nutrient deficiencies or have an infectious parasitic disease called mange. No matter why the gerbils have bald spots, such gerbils should not be purchased.

Facing page and below: *In female gerbils the opening to the vagina is near the anus and almost incorporated into a single hairless area. The scrotum of males is far removed from the anus, making its own hairless patch. Photos by M. Gilroy.*

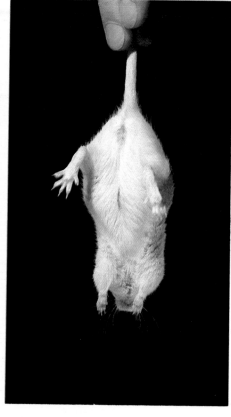

Selecting Breeding Stock

Finally, ask the dealer from whom you intend to purchase the gerbils to feed them. If he normally feeds them at some other time, ask him to let you come back to watch the feeding. If he is a dealer who cares about building his business, he will accommodate your request, and you will then know if the gerbils are feeding normally. If they are not, don't buy them. Starting out with trouble is not the easiest way to become a gerbil breeder.

Until recently, there was little to say about color selection in gerbils, because there was only one color available - agouti, the tannish color described earlier. But as gerbils became more popular and domesticated stock became more readily available, color mutations began to show up.

Facing page: To sex your gerbil, hold it gently but firmly at the base of the tail and then suspend it head-down to inspect the anal area. Photo by G. Axelrod.

One of the first to be developed was the white gerbil. This is just a simple recessive albino mutation - a mutation in which one of the many genes responsible for color has changed. The result is that no pigment appears in the fur, skin or any other part of the animal. The animal is all white in the fur-covered areas, and the areas of bare skin and the eyes are pink. Since the mutation is completely recessive, white gerbils breed true. That is, a white gerbil bred to a white gerbil results in all white offspring. For the beginner, this strain is not recommended, as it tends to be less hardy than the standard agouti or other color forms. This is usually the case with any animal that is of the albino variety. Mutations of almost any sort are rarely simple occurrences. One gene directly or indirectly affects many traits in an organism, not just one trait (as once thought). Often affected in albino animals are some of their internal physiological systems, so they are generally weaker and do not reproduce as well as their normal brethren. Albinos are rarely seen in the wild, for they are highly subject to predation due to their total lack of cryptic coloration.

Another cause of weakness in the albino gerbil is the fact that it is, due to its scarcity, highly inbred. This is a breeding scheme in which brothers and sisters are mated to each other in each generation - a very poor practice in animal husbandry. This inevitably results in deterioration of the strain, because it reveals more and more deleterious genes with each succeeding generation. These faulty genes exist on the chromosomes of almost any organism, but because there are two sets of genes in most animals and the alternate gene at each location is usually normal (or at least not the same as the faulty gene) and often dominant to the

Some people firmly believe that the newer color mutations are not as hardy or as easy to breed as is the plain agouti gerbil. There may be something to this, as the mutants are always heavily inbred, with the chances of faults increasing with inbreeding.

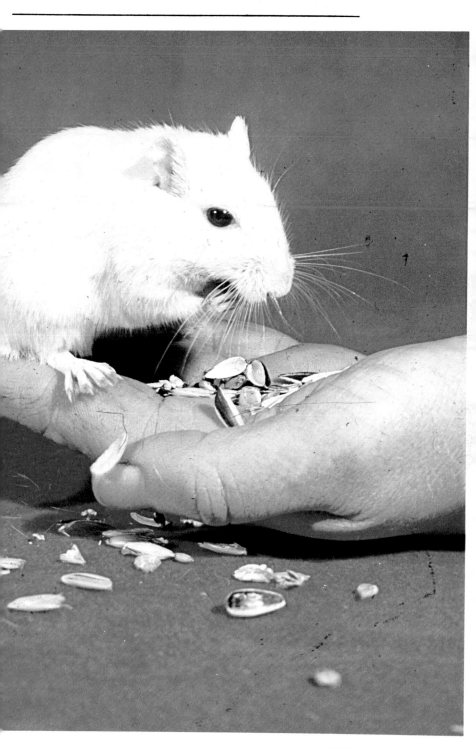

deleterious form, the deleterious form remains masked even though it is successfully passed on from one generation to the next. However, when brothers are mated to sisters the chances of a recessive lethal or sublethal gene being paired with a similar recessive gene are greatly increased.

Above: *You may have to look through several pet shops before you find any of the color mutants for sale. Most shops still sell largely agoutis and perhaps piebalds. To get blacks, ivories, cinnamons, and doves you may have to do some searching. Photo by Dr. Herbert R. Axelrod.*

Black gerbils are one of the latest commercially available strains. These were bred from piebald gerbils, a form having a pattern of black and white patches. Like albinos, blacks are true-breeding. A black bred to a black produces all black offspring (with an occasional small white patch on the throat, chest or forehead). Inbreeding also weakens this strain as it does any other. Unfortunately, it is still almost a necessity, again due to scarcity, to breed black brothers and sisters together to get consistently black offspring.

If two piebald gerbils are bred, or a black and a piebald are bred, some of the offspring will have the normal agouti coloration, some will be brown and white piebald, some will be black and white piebald and some will be black. The wild agouti color seems to be genetically dominant to all of these strains, and usually all agouti offspring are produced when an agouti animal is bred to any of these other color forms.

The genetics of color inheritance in gerbils is not yet well-known because color forms other than agouti have not been known for

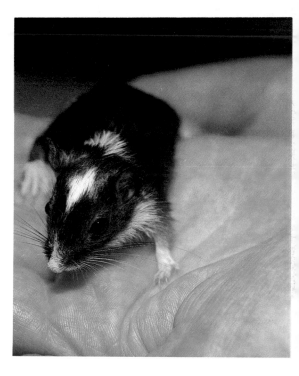

Above: *The white spot pattern is now developed in several colors. In this black baby it is especially distinctive. Photo by M. Gilroy.*

Above: *A black mother and her day-old babies. Unless we know what the father was both genotypically and phenotypically, it is not possible to predict what the babies will look like. Photo by M. Gilroy.*

more than a few years. It is hoped that the smattering of information given here will be helpful in selecting gerbils to give you the results you are after. Until the color genetics of these animals are well-known, it is going to take a lot of trial and error to produce some of the color strains you may want.

While we are on the subject of inheritance, this would be the best time to discuss the specifics of inbreeding in terms of your selection of breeding stock. As mentioned above, inbreeding results in the overt expression of many lethal or sublethal genes that might otherwise continue to remain concealed. In gerbils, continued brother-to-sister matings result in kinked tails, bald patches on the legs and tails, bent spines, deformed teeth and jaws and many other visible anomalies. It also results in numerous less visible anomalies in the reproductive system,

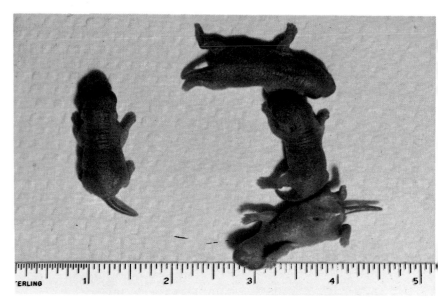

Above: *Very young gerbils. In only three weeks they will be weaned.*

Facing page: *To prevent accidental inbreeding, gerbils must be sexed as early as possible and separated. Photo by M. Gilroy.*

digestive system, nervous system, hormonal system and almost any other physiological internal system of the gerbil. These "inconspicuous" anomalies often produce obvious effects such as poor color, lethargic behavior, poor eating habits and poor reproductive ability.

In order to avoid inbreeding difficulties, brother-to-sister matings should be avoided where possible. When buying your initial stock, for example, a lot of problems can be avoided by buying the males and females from two different sources.

As long as they are young specimens, there usually will be no trouble when they are put together in the same cage. The likelihood of deleterious characteristics such as kinked tails showing up in the offspring from such a mating is remote.

Breeding Behavior

The breeding of gerbils is not very difficult. In fact, under almost any circumstance, if left to themselves they breed without any special conditions being provided for them. In order to be able to selectively breed them at your will rather than their own, however, it is helpful to know something about their reproductive physiology.

The female gerbil has her first heat (or estrus) at the age of 10 to 12 weeks. It does not matter what time of the year the gerbil reaches this age, for gerbils are polyestrous; that is, they come into the period of sexual receptivity (heat) numerous times during the year.

During anestrus, which is the sexually quiescent period between heats, the female shows no sexual interest in the male. As the estrus approaches, hormonal secretions from the pituitary gland stimulate the development of ova

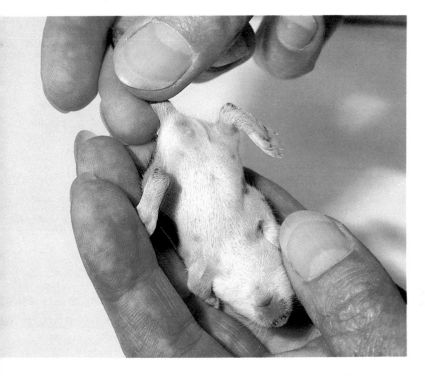

(eggs). Further pituitary secretions produce a group of hormones called estrogens that stimulate the release of ova from the ovaries. Release of the eggs triggers the secretion of other hormones that aid in the preparation of the uterine wall to receive the eggs after they have been fertilized - these hormones are called progestins. If the eggs are not fertilized, the hormonal secretions wane and terminate, and the female gerbil once again goes into quiescent anestrus. However, if the eggs are fertilized they become implanted in the uterine wall where they develop into embryos. As the pregnancy reaches completion, other hormonal secretions stimulate changes in the female that allow for the young to pass through the birth canal and for the female to begin to lactate.

The above description is, of course, a gross oversimplification of the estrous cycle, but understanding it at this elementary level helps the breeder understand why producing good gerbils is not as easy as it seems on first thought. The reproductive process is very complex, and many environmental

Above: *Breeding gerbils on a moderate scale requires a space you can call your own so that you can set up enough cages for both mating pairs and the growing young. To control your stock you must be able to segregate the different colors. Photo by Dr. Herbert R. Axelrod.*

influences such as diet, temperature, humidity, etc., can have profound effects on reproduction at any one of many critical points in the process.

The male gerbil also goes through cyclic periods of hormonal secretion, with the principal male sex hormone being testosterone, which stimulates sperm production. The male also experiences periods of sexual quiescence.

The breeding cycle that usually produces the best results as far as number of offspring is concerned is the one that falls around mid-summer. At about mid-winter reproductivity declines to its lowest seasonally influenced point - sometimes, but not always, meaning no reproduction at all.

It is quite common for a female gerbil to enter the next sexual cycle while she is nursing a litter, and copulation more often than not occurs during that time. This creates no problems for the gerbils, for the young are weaned at about 21 days of age and the gestation period is about 25 to 28 days. If the female has copulated during lactation, she will produce the next litter a

A mixed litter of black, cinnamon, dove, and agouti young. Except when recessive colors are bred to recessve colors, a mixture of colors should be expected in the litters of mixed color parents. Photo by M. Gilroy.

week or two after the last one was weaned.

The female gerbil has a reproductive life of about 15 months. The first pregnancy usually does not produce the most pups. After one or two pregnancies the number of pups per litter can be as high as eight, although five is more common. (A few instances of litters of 12 pups have been recorded, but such occurrences are quite rare.)

The reproductive peak in the female usually occurs at about one year of age. After that the number of pups per litter and the quality of the pups begin to decline. During the declining reproductive period the frequency of pregnancies drops also. A female gerbil bears an average of about seven litters during her reproductive life. The average reproductive life of a male is about 20 months, with his peak occurring at about the same time as that of the female or sometimes a little bit later. It is not uncommon for a male

gerbil to be sexually active for many months after a female has lost her ability to reproduce and has lost all interest in sexual activity.

Copulation in gerbils is not a simple affair. For a successful copulation to occur the female must be estrous or in heat and the male must be at the peak of his sexual cycle. Thumping is an intricate part of the courtship ritual. The male crowds the female and both animals sniff each other's genital areas. The male then produces anywhere from two to ten thumping series. If the female is sexually receptive, she crouches low on her forelegs and presents her hindquarters to the male. The male mounts the female and thrusts numerous times, but ejaculation does not occur. The male dismounts and sometimes thumps again. The male again mounts and produces multiple thrusts. Ejaculation still does not occur. This process must be repeated about ten times before ejaculation can occur. From observations made in many laboratories it appears that ejaculation in gerbils is not possible until there have been about ten intromissions (penetrations). The male mentioned earlier, the animals use the husks of seeds and dried plant fibers to build the nest. They will chew up any fibrous material you provide for them and use it as nesting material. Ideal items are pieces of cloth or even

Above: *Mating gerbils. Gerbils will intermate regardless of color as long as they are all the same species. Photo by M. Gilroy.*

does not always dismount and thump between intromissions.

Once fertilization and placental implantation have occurred, nest-building activities by both the male and the female become much more intense. As sheets of cotton. In fact, there is a product available at pet shops that is sold as nesting material; consisting of a mat of cotton impregnated with wood chips, it is eagerly torn apart, fluffed up and worked into the nest. Dry wood shavings from the bottom of the cage will also be used. Some people provide their gerbils with empty paper towel rolls or toilet paper rolls to play with. These are also shredded by the gerbils and used as nesting material.

The poorly developed young are born naked (without fur) and with dens. This may be contrasted with animals such as antelope, horses, deer, wildebeest or other savannah grazers that have precocial young (young that are able to run about and take care of themselves, except for

their eyes closed. Each is about the size of a small peanut (in its shell) and is totally helpless. The poor development and helplessness are usually the case with mammals that live and nest in concealed places such as burrows or

Above: *It is probably best to remove toys such as paper tubes from the cage in which mating gerbils are kept. The temptation to play may be too much for them.*

nursing, almost from the moment of birth).

During the nursing period a dietary change for the female can be helpful. She should receive a greater proportion of fats, calcium and phosphorus. This can be done by increasing the number of sunflower seeds and fresh vegetables given - but only a slight increase is necessary.

After a few days the pups begin to crawl about in the nest, and their fur begins to develop. At about ten days they make some feeble attempts to crawl out of the nest. By 15 days of age their eyes are usually open, and it becomes increasingly difficult at this stage for the female to keep the young in the nest. The male often helps round up the young, generally by pushing or shoving them back toward the nest. Rather than actually going after the pup that has wandered away, the male may merely warn the female that her pup is in trouble. In my own lab I once observed a pup wander from the nest (which happened in this case to be on the surface of the soil) and fall down into the burrow. The father came to the edge of the burrow, peered in and ran back to the nursing female. He repeated this behavior pattern over and over again. The female finally pushed her sucklings aside, ran to the burrow, picked up the pup with her teeth, carried it back to the nest and immediately resumed nursing.

Right: New-born gerbils are not an impressive sight as they lack hair and are blind. In just a few days they will be crawling about the nest, however. Photo by P. Bartley.

Selective Breeding

To this point I have discouraged inbreeding in order to minimize heritable defects in gerbils. However, in order to breed selectively to fix, enhance or improve a particular quality, inbreeding is a necessary evil.

As explained earlier, breeding close relatives together increases the chances of lethal, sublethal or otherwise deleterious characteristics being expressed in the offspring. However, the very same inbreeding also offers the opportunity to fix and improve traits. Thus it would seem that the best way to fix a desirable trait is to breed brothers and sisters, each carrying that trait, to one another. While this offers the greatest probability of establishing that trait, it also offers the greatest probability of establishing undesirable traits as well.

The chances of establishing undesirable traits are lessened somewhat by breeding offspring back to their parents instead of to each other. But this also decreases the probability of establishing the desired trait. In a parent-to-offspring mating, however, the chances of the offspring having both the desirable and the undesirable traits at the same time are less than they are in a brother-to-sister mating.

To fix a desirable trait, a typical breeding scheme could be as follows. Start by mating a totally unrelated pair. These are known as the P (parental) generation. From their offspring, which are known as the F1 (first filial) generation, pick the best F1 male and mate it back to the parental female, and mate the best F1 female back to the parental male. This dual mating now establishes two breeding lines in the F2 generation, line A and line B. From the F2A offspring, choose the best male and mate it

A female dove gerbil with her litter. Photo by M. Gilroy.

back to its mother, the F1 female. From the F2B offspring, choose the best female and mate it back to its father, the F1 male. This produces the F3 offspring in line A and in line B.

If no weaknesses have shown up, the parent-to-offspring backcrossing can continue for at least one more generation. Mate the best F3 female from line A back to its father, which is the F2 male of line A. Also mate the best F3 male of line B to its mother, which is line B F2 female; thus the F4 generation is established in each line. By this time heritable anomalies may begin to show up, but these can be quickly wiped out by crossing the two lines. In other words, mate your best F4 female from line A to your best F4 male from line B. This establishes two new lines and the parent-to-offspring backcrosses can continue for at least another three generations before the linecrossing must be repeated.

If the quality of your stock continues to decline after the first linecrossing, and it's very possible that it could, it is best then to introduce new stock from another source as one parent in each line, and it won't take very long to re-establish the high-quality trait you were breeding for.

Preselection of mates by the breeder does not always work. When strange gerbils are introduced into the same cage fights often ensue, resulting in some pretty serious injuries and sometimes even the death of the weaker gerbil. For introducing the initial stock this is not usually a problem if young gerbils (not more than two months of age) are selected. For subsequent offspring-to-parent matings this problem can be overcome by allowing the young to grow for about two months in the presence of the parents; then, one by one, every few days remove those offspring that will not be selected and remove the one parent that will not be used. This scheme usually works well if the parent is removed first. In the case of the first generation cross where both parents will be used to establish two breeding lines, divide the latter in half, separating each parent with the selected offspring and with one water soluble. A particular spot on the body is chosen for the mark. For esthetic reasons the spot chosen is usually some inconspicuous place such as behind the ear or even inside the ear. One problem with dye marks, however, is that

or two others if they are available. Then, after a few days, start removing the undesired offspring.

One problem that often arises when selecting offspring for the breeding plan is telling them apart consistently, time after time. Without some sort of marking system, the wrong gerbil could be mistakenly removed from the cage. There are all sorts of dye markers available. Some people even use felt-tip pens having ink that is not

Above: *Be sure to carefully inspect the parents and offspring regularly during any breeding program. Unexpected flaws may develop as the animals age. Photo by R. Hanson.*

very few dye systems are permanent. One permanent marking system is to make a very tiny notch on the outer edge of the gerbil's ear. This is done with a small fingernail clipper. The notch should not be any more than one-sixteenth of an inch deep (less if possible). No blood will be drawn if the notch is not made any deeper than this, and it will not inflict pain on the gerbil either, since there are hardly any nerve endings at the outer edge of the ear.

My final suggestion for selective breeding is that you always keep your eyes open for the possibility of developing a new strain. This is how the black, piebald and albino gerbils were developed - a keen-eyed breeder saw these mutations arise and, following the above or some other suitable mating scheme, fixed a brand new color strain. In guinea pigs, mice and hamsters we have seen the development of a variety of fur types as well as color patterns. Long-haired and curly-haired guinea pigs and hamsters, each in a variety of colors, are not all that uncommon and they, too, arose as the result of an observant breeder.

Last, but not least, I would like to offer one more piece of advice. Don't count your gerbils before they are born. In other words, enjoy breeding your gerbils and enjoy improving your strains. If you happen to make a little bit of money along the way, so much the better. Perhaps you can even make enough to offset all of your costs in the hobby of gerbil breeding. But don't look upon gerbil-breeding as a get-rich-quick scheme. To begin with, there are a number of well-established small animal farms that are capable of providing most pet shops with all the gerbils they can possibly use, and at a much lower cost than you as an amateur breeder can produce them for. Secondly, once gerbil-breeding becomes a way of making a living, there is very little time to enjoy it as a hobby, and eventually you will probably lose interest in gerbil-breeding as a hobby altogether. So enjoy breeding your gerbils. Who knows, you may be the developer of the first angora gerbils!

Health Care

Gerbils are naturally hardy animals and will live a normal healthy life provided you offer a well-balanced diet and maintain a clean, dry, draft-free environment for them. Gerbils may develop digestive disorders if there is a lack of roughage in their diet or if the diet is over-rich in fats and carbohydrates. (Remember not to overfeed your gerbil with sunflower seeds!) Similarly, too many soft vegetables may cause gastro-intestinal upsets along with diarrhea. Perishable foods (such as vegetables) should be offered sparingly and removed from the gerbil's cage if not readily eaten, since spoiled food may be contaminated with bacteria or other deleterious agents that cause disease to spread.

Proper storage of foods is important; dry foods and pellets should be kept in sealed containers that are vermin- and moisture-proof and vegetables and soft foods should be kept refrigerated.

Unlike many other rodents, gerbils are not carriers of infectious diseases such as rabies. Most diseases and disorders which affect gerbils have a direct relationship with improper food handling and poor housing management by the gerbil owner. In order to keep your gerbil free of illness, it is up to you to

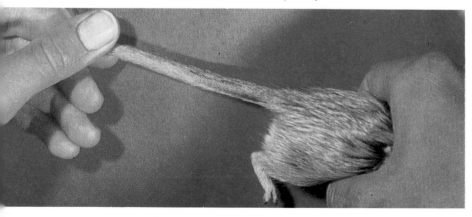

exercise the necessary preventive measures of removing those conditions which may cause problems to occur. Colds, for example, may be prevented by providing your gerbil with warm, dry cage litter and by placing the gerbil's cage far from drafty areas. Diarrhea can be avoided by offering green vegetables in moderation and by removing spoiled food from the cage.

A healthy gerbil will be active and playful. Its fur will be soft and sleek; its eyes will be bright, clear and curious. Signs of illness to watch for are: listlessness, unresponsiveness to you, ruffled fur, anorexia (loss of appetite), diarrhea, and runny nose or eyes. Whenever you suspect a problem, it is best to consult your veterinarian, who will offer advice and/or prescribe a treatment for your pet. In many instances, a daily observation of your pet gerbil will allow you to control most of these conditions before they become unmanageable.

Below: *No problems!* Photo by S. A. Thompson.

Index

A young pair of fancy colored gerbils, a male agouti Canadian white spot and a black female. Photo by M. Gilroy.

A COMPLETE INTRODUCTION TO
GERBILS